TOOLS FOR CAREGIVERS

- **F&P LEVEL:** A
- **WORD COUNT:** 17
- **CURRICULUM CONNECTIONS:** animals, habitats, nature

Skills to Teach

- **HIGH-FREQUENCY WORDS:** a, is, it
- **CONTENT WORDS:** climbs, eats, grabs, koala, rides, sleeps, walks
- **PUNCTUATION:** exclamation point, periods
- **WORD STUDY:** /k/, spelled c (*climbs*); long /e/, spelled ea (*eats*); long /e/, spelled ee (*sleeps*)
- **TEXT TYPE:** information report

Before Reading Activities

- Read the title and give a simple statement of the main idea.
- Have students "walk" through the book and talk about what they see in the pictures.
- Introduce new vocabulary by having students predict the first letter and locate the word in the text.
- Discuss any unfamiliar concepts that are in the text.

After Reading Activities

Koalas are built to live in trees. They even eat leaves! If readers could be an animal, where would they live? Would they choose to live in the trees, in the water, or in the air? As an animal, what would they need to live in their habitat? Ask readers to draw themselves as an animal in a specific habitat. Have each reader share their answer and drawing with the group.

Tadpole Books are published by Jump!, 5357 Penn Avenue South, Minneapolis, MN 55419, www.jumplibrary.com
Copyright ©2024 Jump!. International copyright reserved in all countries. No part of this book may be reproduced in any form without written permission from the publisher.
Editor: Jenna Gleisner   **Designer:** Emma Almgren-Bersie
Photo Credits: Eric Isselee/Shutterstock, cover, 1, 2mr, 12–13; GlobalP/iStock, 2tl, 6–7; jeep2499/Shutterstock, 2tr, 10–11; D. Parer & E. Parer-Cook/Minden Pictures/SuperStock, 2ml, 8–9; Bildagentur Zoonar GmbH/Shutterstock, 2bl, 14–15; quentinjlang/iStock, 2br, 4–5; Maridav/iStock, 3; LouieLea/Shutterstock, 16.
Library of Congress Cataloging-in-Publication Data
Names: Deniston, Natalie, author.
Title: Koalas / by Natalie Deniston.
Description: Minneapolis, MN: Jump!, Inc., (2024)
Series: My first animal books | Includes index.
Audience: Ages 3–6
Identifiers: LCCN 2022054040 (print)
LCCN 2022054041 (ebook)
ISBN 9798885246675 (hardcover)
ISBN 9798885246682 (paperback)
ISBN 9798885246699 (ebook)
Subjects: LCSH: Koala—Juvenile literature.
Classification: LCC QL737.M384 D46 2024 (print)
LCC QL737.M384 (ebook)
DDC 599.2/5—dc23/eng/20221110
LC record available at https://lccn.loc.gov/2022054040
LC ebook record available at https://lccn.loc.gov/2022054041

MY FIRST ANIMAL BOOKS

KOALAS

by Natalie Deniston

TABLE OF CONTENTS

Words to Know 2

Koalas 3

Let's Review! 16

Index 16

WORDS TO KNOW

climbs

eats

grabs

rides

sleeps

walks

KOALAS

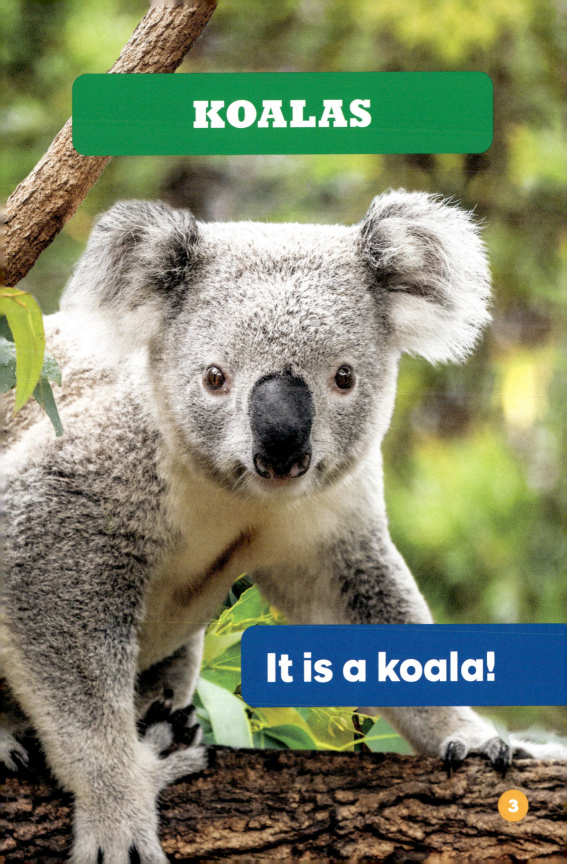

It is a koala!

It walks.

It climbs.

claw

It grabs.

It eats.

It rides.

It sleeps.

LET'S REVIEW!

What is this koala doing?

INDEX

climbs 7
eats 11
grabs 9

rides 13
sleeps 15
walks 5